MY MOM IS A WORRY WART

WRITTEN BY KAREN SNYDER

ILLUSTRATED BY NATALIA LARGUIER

Copyright © 2024 Karen Snyder

All rights reserved. No part of this publication may be reproduced, distributed, or transmitted in any form or by any means, including photocopying, recording, or other electronic or mechanical methods, without the prior written permission of the publisher, except as permitted by U.S. copyright law. For permission requests, contact publisher/author.

www.authorksnyder.com

ISBN: 979-8-9911481-0-8 (Hardcover)

ISBN: 979-8-9911481-1-5 (ebook)

Library of Congress Control Number: 2024915502

The story, all names, characters, and incidents portrayed in this production are fictitious. No identification with actual persons (living or deceased), places, buildings, and products is intended or should be inferred.

Book Cover by Natalia Larguier

Illustrations by Natalia Larguier

Creative Consulting by Jennifer Asaro

Editing by Melissa Richeson & Mark Asaro

Proofreader Christie Hainsby

Printed in China

First printing edition 2024

This is to all the worrywart moms and the kids who adore them, and for the women who have inspired and fretted over me.

To *Antoniette*, my great grandmother, who courageously crossed the ocean to give her future children a better life and her daughter, my grandmother, Louise, a talented author and lyricist who always motivated me to follow my creative interests.

To my exceptional mom *Barbara*, a military wife who raised 5 accomplished kids while my hero dad, Henry, ensured our safety.

To my amazing daughter, *Jennifer*, a successful career woman and strong defender and supporter of her son Sebastian, who has motivated me to write children's books promoting diversity, inclusivity, and acceptance.

I also want to give a special shout-out to *Megan*, my daughter from another mother, who I know will one day make an amazing mom, and to my guys - *Michael*, *Ian*, *Mark*, and *Alex* - for always being there for me with their love and support.

Finally, I am deeply grateful to my extraordinary husband *Michael* for his unwavering support and for always having my back and being a sounding board for all my crazy ideas.

Thank you all for the love, joy, and countless gray hairs I've gained as the ultimate worrywart mom!

My mom is the world's biggest worrywart!

Which means she's a fun-wrecker and spoilsport.

Like a hummingbird or a bumblebee,

she's always busy buzzing over me.

My mom is a worrywart!

. At the park, it's really embarrassing

when my mom starts her nonstop parenting.

"Be careful, Grace, or you're gonna get hurt.

Please stay on the sand and avoid the dirt.

Don't run or you'll fall,

and don't climb on trees,

and button up—I think I feel a breeze.

If Mom had her way, I'd never leave home. She'd crown me a queen and buy me a throne.

Then she'd keep watch in front of the castle,
with the Queen's guards in headgear and tassel.
Red coat, gold buttons, and shiny black shoes,
searching for danger, on the hunt for clues.

Sometimes Mom's caring can be kind of nice—

a load of sugar with a lump of spice.

But she can't protect me from every blow,

or bubble pack me up from head to toe.

So ease off the brakes, Mom, and let me roam,

'cause I'm a big girl now. I'm almost grown!

When I'm all grown up, I'll earn a degree in a famous college across the sea.

I'll invite the princess for proper tea, with my pinkies up, just like Mom taught me.

I'll join the circus and wear a top hat,

and soar in the air like an acrobat.

Then hop aboard the Orient Express,

in my sparkly shoes and fanciest dress.

In Africa, I'll join a safari,

And meet lions in the Kalahari.

Then, team up with a group of wildebeest,

While guiding a river raft heading east.

My handy compass will keep me on track,

As I sled through snow with a fierce wolf pack.

Once I stake my claim on the highest peak,

I'll take a deep breath and let out a shriek.

"Hello! Hello! Can you hear me below?"

My voice will soar on the wings of a crow,

across the mountain and over the sea.

A message by airmail to Mom from me.

Whew! Oh my goodness! That was a close call!

Good thing Mom was watching me after all!

Using her Mom Power, she saved the day!

With magic kisses, my tears went away.

My boo-boos quickly disappeared from sight,

but then a lecture that lasted all night

and started again in the morning light.

"Grace, I love hearing of all that you'll do.

You know, I was once a little girl too.

But give yourself time to grow and blossom,

'cause being a kid is super awesome!"

"Now, let's get going, or you'll miss the bus.

No dilly-dallying or making a fuss.

And today I've made your favorite lunch:

PB & J, and a fruity fruit punch.

But before we leave..."

"...pick up your dirty towels from the floor,

and please put my lipstick back in the drawer.

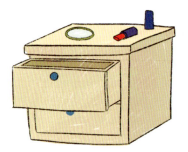

Be sure to brush your teeth and scrub your neck,

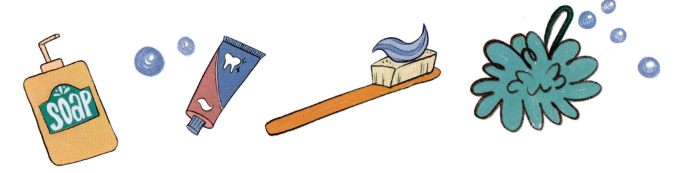

and straighten your room because it's a wreck!

Tie your shoelaces, and let's comb your hair.

"...make sure you're wearing clean underwear."

"Mom, come on! Clean underwear? Of course I'm wearing clean underwear!"

"Yes, Grace, I know you're a big girl now."

"Oh, Mom, you're so embarrassing!"

"I love you, Grace."

"I love you too, Mom."

As it turns out, Mom's a pretty good sport.

Even though she's the biggest worrywart.

I still think she should get the Best-Mom prize,

for always being so caring and wise.

And I'm so lucky that my mom is mine,

'cause I have

THE GREATEST MOM

OF ALL TIME!